Valentines

— ❦ —

A Book of Quotations

It is difficult to know at what moment love begins;
it is less difficult to know that it has begun.
Henry Wadsworth Longfellow

Who ever loved, that loved not at first sight.

Christopher Marlowe

The first duty of love is to listen.

Paul Tillich

The lover knows much more about absolute good and universal beauty than any logician or theologian, unless the latter, too, be lovers in disguise.

George Santayana

And Steal immortal blessings from her lips;
who, even in pure and vestal modesty,
still blush, as thinking their own kisses sin.
William Shakespeare, Romeo and Juliet

You may conquer with a sword
but you are conquered by a kiss.
Daniel Heinsius

A beauty is a woman you notice;
A charmer is one who notices you.
Adlai Stevenson

I date this girl for two years – and then the nagging
starts: "I wanna know your name."
Mike Binder

Love is the answer, but while you're waiting
for the answer, sex raises some pretty good questions.
Woody Allen

I steal a kiss from her sleeping shadow moves.
'Cause I'll always miss her wherever she goes.
And I'll always need her more than she could ever need me.
I need someone to ease my mind,
but sometimes a someone is so hard to find.

Billy Corgan

You have to walk carefully in the beginning of love;
the running across fields into your lover's arms
can only come later when you're sure
they won't laugh if you trip.
Jonathan Carroll, Outside the Dog Museum

A kiss is the shortest distance between two people.

Henry Youngman

Nimble thought can jump both sea and land.

William Shakespeare

Put away the book, the description, the tradition, the authority, and take the journey of self-discovery. Love, and don't be caught in opinions and ideas about what love is or should be. When you love, everything will come right. Love has its own action. Love, and you will know the blessings of it. Keep away from the authority who tells you what love is and what it is not. No authority knows and he who knows cannot tell. Love, and there is understanding.

Krishnamurti

Never be possessive. If a female friend lets on that she is going out with another man, be kind and understanding. If she says she would like to go out with the Dallas Cowboys, including the coaching staff, the same rule applies. Tell her: "Kath, you just go right ahead and do what you feel is right." Unless you actually care for her, in which case you must see to it that she has no male contact whatsoever.

Bruce Jay Friedman

If I were a girl, I'd despair.
The supply of good women far exceeds that
of the men who deserve them.

Robert Graves

Never judge someone by who he's in love with;
judge him by his friends. People fall in love
with the most appalling people. Take a cool,
appraising glance at his pals.

Cynthia Heimel

Love does not consist in gazing at each other,
but in looking outward together in the same direction.

Antoine de Saint-Exupéry

If a relationship is to evolve, it must go through
a series of endings.

Lisa Moriyama

We cannot really love anybody
with whom we never laugh.
Agnes Repplier

Love is like the measles.
The older you get it, the worse the attack.
Mary Roberts Rhinehart

I love a hand that meets my own with a grasp
that causes some sensation.

Samuel Osgood

Whenever I date a guy, I think, is this the man
I want my children to spend their weekends with?

Rita Rudner

The most exciting attractions are between
two opposites that never meet.
Andy Warhol

That is the best – to laugh with someone because
you think the same things are funny.
Gloria Vanderbilt

With the catching end the pleasures of the chase.

Abraham Lincoln

People who throw kisses are mighty, hopelessly lazy.

Bob Hope

If you haven't had at least a slight poetic crack
in the heart, you have been cheated by nature.
Phyllis Battelle

The great tragedy of life is not that men perish,
but that they cease to love.

W Somerset Maugham

Soul meets soul on lovers lips.

Percy Shelley

With a kiss let us set out for an unknown world.

Alfred de Musset

The universe hangs on a kiss,
exists in the hold of a kiss.
Zalman Shneor

I never wanted to weigh more heavily on a man
than a bird.

Gabrielle ("Coco") Chanel,
on why she never married her lovers

The face of a lover is an unknown, precisely because
it is invested with so much of oneself.
It is a mystery, containing, like all mysteries,
the possibility of torment.

James Baldwin

I met in the street a very poor young man who was in love. His hat was old, his coat worn, his cloak was out at the elbows, the water passed through his shoes, – and the stars through his soul.

Victor Hugo

There is no surprise more magical than the surprise of being loved: It is God's finger on man's shoulder.

Charles Morgan

To cheat oneself out of love is the most terrible deception; it is an eternal loss for which there is no reparation, either in time or in eternity.

Soren Kierkegaard

At the touch of Love everyone becomes a poet.

Plato

The course of true love never did run smooth.

William Shakespeare

Love vanquishes time. To lovers, a moment
can be eternity, eternity can be the tick of a clock.
Mary Parrish

Those have most power to hurt us, that we love.

Francis Beaumont and John Fletcher,
from The Maid's Tragedy

Falling in love is so powerful that it makes you
want to forget about everything else . . .
Instead of wanting to struggle and destroy things,
you want to find peace and to celebrate living.

Anchee Min

He who binds to himself a joy
Does the winged life destroy;
But he who kisses the joy as it flies
Lives in eternity's sunrise.

William Blake

Love is an attempt to change a piece
of a dream world into reality.

Theodor Reik

Quarrels in France strengthen a love affair,
in America they end it.

Ned Rorem

Love, all alike, no season knows, nor clime,
Nor hours, age, months, which are the rags of time.

John Donne

Few men know how to kiss well.
Fortunately, I've always had time to teach them.
Mae West

A kiss, when all is said, what is it?
An oath that's given closer than before;
A promise more precise; the sealing of
Confessions that till then were barely breathed;
A rosy dot placed on the i in loving.

Edmond Rostand

Love can be understood only "from the inside,"
as a language can be understood only by someone
who speaks it, as a world can be understood
only by someone who lives in it.

Robert C Solomon

You have to kiss a lot of toads before you find
a handsome prince.

American Proverb

She will never win him, whose
Words had shown she feared to lose.
Dorothy Parker

There is nothing holier, in this life of ours,
than the first consciousness of love –
the first fluttering of its silken wings.
Henry Wadsworth Longfellow

A kiss can be a comma, a question mark
or an exclamation point. That's basic spelling
that every woman ought to know.

Mistinguett

Lovers may be, and indeed, generally are enemies,
but they can never be friends.

Lord Bryon

How great love is, presence best trial makes,
But absence tries how long this love will be.
John Donne

A true lover always feels in debt to the one he loves.

Ralph W Sockman

Kisses: Words which cannot be written.

Nicole Louise Divino

Love looks not with the eyes, but with the mind;
And therefore is winged Cupid painted blind.
William Shakespeare, A Midsummer Night's Dream,

The Lord watch between me and thee
when we are absent from one another.

Genesis 31:49

A long, long kiss, – a kiss of youth and love.

Lord Byron

Lips only sing when they cannot kiss.

James Thomson

Courtesy wins woman all as well
As valour may, but he that closes both
Is perfect.

Alfred, Lord Tennyson

The ineffable joy of forgiving and being forgiven
forms an ecstasy that might well arouse
the envy of the gods.

Elbert Hubbard

Love is, above all, the gift of oneself.

Jean Anouilh

A legal kiss is never as good as a stolen one.

Guy de Maupassant

Love reckons hours for months, and days for years;
every little absence is an age.

John Dryden

What is uttered from the heart alone
Will win the hearts of others to your own.
Johann Wolfgang von Goethe

Though seas and land betwixt us both
Our faith and troth,
Like separated souls,
All time and space controls:
Above the highest sphere we meet,
Unseen, unknown; and greet as angels greet.

Richard Lovelace

The fountains mingle with the river
And the rivers with the Ocean,
The winds of heaven mix for ever
With a sweet emotion;
Nothing in the world is single;
All things by a law divine
In one spirit meet and mingle,
Why not I with thine?

Shelley

'My soul is so knit to yours that it is
but a divided life I live without you.'
Dinah from Adam Bede by George Eliot

I wasn't kissing her,
I was whispering in her mouth.
Chico Maroc

The magic of first love is our ignorance
that it can ever end.
Benjamin Disraeli

The man who has never made a fool of himself
in love will never be wise in love.

Theodor Reik

We two form a multitude.

Author Unidentified

The love we give away is the only love we keep.

Elbert Hubbard

Ancient lovers believed a kiss would literally unite
their souls, because the spirit was said to be carried
in one's breath.

Eve Glicksman

This swift business
I must uneasy make, lest too light winning
Make the prize light.

William Shakespeare: The Tempest

The return makes one love the farewell.

Alfred de Musset

In love, pain and pleasure are always at war.
Publilius Syrus

We are all born for love;
it is the principle of existence and its only end.
Benjamin Disraeli

Let us always meet each other with smile,
for the smile is the beginning of love
Mother Teresa

The sound of a kiss is much softer than that of a cannon – but it's echo lasts a great deal longer.

Anonymous

We kiss. And it feels like we have just shrugged off the world.

Jim Shahin

For every beauty there is an eye somewhere to see it.
For every truth there is an ear somewhere to hear it.
For every love there is a heart somewhere to receive it.

Ivan Panin

Love has features which pierce all hearts,
he wears a bandage which conceals the faults of those beloved.
He has wings, he comes quickly and flies away the same.

Voltaire

Come to me in my dreams, and then,
By day I shall be well again,
For then the night will more than pay
The hopeless longing of the day.

Matthew Arnold

When love beckons to you, follow him,
Though his ways are hard and steep.
And when his wings enfold you yield to him,
Though the sword hidden among his pinions
may wound you.

Kahlil Gibran

You may conquer with the sword,
but you are conquered by a kiss.
Daniel Heinsius

Love is the difficult realisation that something
other than oneself is real.

Iris Murdoch

Music is love in search of a word.

Sidney Lanier

Happiness and love are just a choice away.

Leo Buscaglia

To fear love is to fear life.

Bertrand Russell

They do not love that do not show their love.

William Shakespeare, The Two Gentlemen of Verona

If it is your time love will track you down
like a cruise missile. If you say "No! I don't want it
right now," that's when you'll get it for sure.
Love will make a way out of no way.
Love is an exploding cigar which we willingly smoke.

Lynda Barry

The truth is that there is only one terminal dignity – love.
And the story of a love is not important –
what is important is that one is capable of love.
It is perhaps the only glimpse we are permitted of eternity.

Helen Hayes

Love is the poetry of the senses.

Honore de Balzac

The loving are the daring.

Bayard Taylor

We can only learn to love by loving.

Iris Murdoch

Love is the enchanted dawn of every heart.

Alphonse de Lamartine

The beginning of love is to let those we love
be perfectly themselves, and not to twist them to fit
our own image. Otherwise we love only
the reflection of ourselves we find in them.

Thomas Merton

A bell's not a bell 'til you ring it
A song's not a song 'til you sing it
Love in your heart wasn't put there to stay
Love isn't love 'til you give it away!

Oscar and Hammerstein

Love is a pure dew which drops from heaven
into our heart, when God wills.

Arsene Houssaye

To love someone is to see a miracle
invisible to others.

François Mauriac

If you would be loved, love and be lovable.

Benjamin Franklin

Love sought is good, but given unsought is better.

William Shakespeare, Twelfth Night

Love and electricity are one in the same, my dear . . .
if you do not feel the jolt in your soul every time
a kiss is shared, a whisper is spoken, a touch is felt,
then you're not really in love at all . . .

C J Franks

To the Tin Man:
". . . remember, my sentimental friend, that a heart is not judged by how much you love, but by how much you are loved, by others."

Frank Morgan as the Wizard of Oz

Then they looked at each other,
not quite as they had looked before, for in their eyes
there was the memory of a kiss.

from Adam Bede by George Eliot

Do not think that love, in order to be genuine, has to be extraordinary. What we need is to love without getting tired.

Mother Teresa

By starlight, I'll kiss you,
and promise to be your one and only.
I'll make you feel happy and leave you
to be lost in mine.

Billy Corgan

Love is not some complex, mystical abstraction.
It is something accessible and human that we learn
through our everyday experience, as often at times
of failure as in moments of ecstasy.

Leo Buscaglia

Forgiveness is the final form of love.

Reinhold Niebuhr

Love and you shall be loved.

Ralph Waldo Emerson

A loving heart is the truest wisdom.

Charles Dickens

Gravity is not responsible for people falling in love.

Albert Einstein

The way to love anything is to realise
that it might be lost.
Gilbert K Chesterton

The naked promise in a glance,
the electricity in a touch, the delicious heat in a kiss . . .
Trudy Culross

How bold one gets when one is sure of being loved!

Sigmund Freud

Seek first to understand, then to be understood.

Stephen Covey

Some women blush when they are kissed,
some call for the police, some swear, some bite.
But the worst are those who laugh.

William Raye

O Love, O fire! Once he drew
With one long kiss my whole soul through.
My lips, as sunlight drinketh dew.

Alfred, Lord Tennyson

The less you open your heart to others,
the more your heart suffers.

Deepak Chopra

Platonic friendship: The interval between
the introduction and the first kiss.

Sophie Irene Loeb

So, so, break off this last lamenting kiss,
Which sucks two souls and vapours both away.

John Donne

All, everything that I understand,
I understand only because I love.
Leo Tolstoy, War and Peace

To love deeply in one direction makes us
more loving in all others.

Madame Swetchine

To love is the great Amulet
that makes this world a garden.
Robert Louis Stevenson

A soft lip would tempt you to an eternity of kissing.

Ben Jonson

Love comforteth like sunshine after rain.

William Shakespeare

Was this the face that launch'd a thousand ships
and burnt the topless towers of Ilium?
Sweet Helen, make me immortal with a kiss!
Her lips suck forth my soul: see where it flies!
Christopher Marlowe: Doctor Faustus

No, this trick won't work . . .
How on earth are you ever going to explain in terms
of chemistry and physics so important a biological
phenomenon as first love?

Albert Einstein

What of soul was left, I wonder, when the kissing
had to stop?

Robert Browning

Love is a sport in which the hunter must contrive
to have the quarry in pursuit.

Alphonse Kerr

I never knew how much like heaven this world could be,
when two people love and live for one another!
from Good Wives by Louisa M Alcott

Love may not make the world go round,
but I must admit that it makes the ride worthwhile.

Sean Connery

Love is an irresistible desire to be irresistibly desired.

Robert Frost

Kisses are a better fate than wisdom.

E E Cummings

Love – the feeling – is a fruit of love, the verb.

Stephen Covey

Love is but the discovery of ourselves in others,
and the delight in the recognition.
Alexander Smith

Treasure each other in the recognition
that we do not know how long we shall have each other.
Joshua Loth Liebman

For one man is my world of all the men
This wide world holds;
O love, my world is you.

Christina Rossetti

Today I begin to understand what love must be,
if it exists . . . When we are parted, we each feel
the lack of the other half of ourselves.
We are incomplete like a book in two volumes
of which the first has been lost. That is what I imagine
love to be: incompleteness in absence.

Goncourt